First Feline

by

Mort Gerberg

ZEBRA BOOKS/KENSINGTON PUBLISHING CORP.

ZEBRA BOOKS
are published by
Kensington Publishing Corp.
475 Park Avenue South
New York, NY 10016

First Printing: January, 1993
Printed in the United States of America

To Judith, Lilia and Pixie
And to new beginnings

Hi. I'm the First Feline and I'll be living in Washington, D.C. with the new First Family. Which is great because for too long now, the White House has been going to the dogs.

The dream came true at 10:58 on Election Night when Dan Purrther and Catty Chung announced it on the all-Mews network.

A little while later I received my first congratulatory phone call, from one of the foremost world renowned figures.

The campaign had been like a full feline fight, with screeching, hissing, scratching, biting, caterwauling, spitting, pouncing, yowling and clawing. Imagine! And the cat-idates weren't even *cats!*

It was very stressful, constantly hearing varied reports about percentages of voters' preferences. I shouldn't have been nervous, though. Who could ever trust *pole*-cats?

The Republicats had hounded me doggedly. Like that search through my records they made just before Election Day. They were scratching around looking for some dirt in my pussport— like a catamaran trip to Catalina, or an Americat Airlines visit to Katmandu. All they could cough up, though, was a fur ball. It was a-mewsing.

Evidence of other illicit probing were those wiretaps found in my bathroom box. Investigators are calling this one "Littergate."

They'd also raised dead issues, like catnip. Well, I admit that in my youth I once tried it—but I didn't inhale.

(Which reminds me that there are reports that the former vice-president was said to have potted around a bit. To him, I suggest that the way to handle it is to just say Noe.)

As for the draft dodging accusations, this is a cat-egoric denial. The Republicats were just being catty. Truth is, the Army wouldn't have me. Simple genetics. Cats are born to *not* take orders or do anything on anybody else's command.

Campaigning across the country was grueling. My stomach couldn't take those long bus rides. More than once we had to stop or there would have been a major cat-astrophe.

Now, though, I sleep peacefully. But if I ever have trouble dozing off, I merely re-count electoral votes.

Out on the street, on November 5th, you could tell just by looking at them which was a Democat and which was a Republicat.

After the election I was so happy, I played all the time. Up until January 20th, every day I would take a bath with my rubber lame ducky.

Two weeks after Election Day I was cat-apulted into the celebrity spotlight. I did absolutely nothing to win this attention. Being a cat, nothing is what I do. And what I plan to continue doing.

The media, with all its snooping cameras, puss-nal questions and nosy recorders, rubs my fur the wrong way. My idea of a good sound bite is on the back of a hand, just above the thumb.

Nevertheless, I realize I must be concerned with projecting an appropriate image. Which makes me wonder how the political cat-oonists will cat-icature me.

I'm actually a very ordinary cat—but I'm in the company of extraordinary people. Like, I've got the normal number of nine lives—but that's not as many as The Main Man's in his political career.

I love playing games with the First Family. One of my favorites is cat's cradle. Another is one o' cat. But I still can't stand the idea of Checkers in the White House.

In an interview by Kitty Kelly in *Catsmopolitan* Magazine, they cat-alog my other favorite things. Here are a few—for now. (Remember, I'm constitutionally finicky.)

Athlete	Catfish Hunter
Astrological Sign	Pisces
Musical	"Cats" (what else?)
Vacation spot	Catskill Mountains
Movie	"Catablanca"; "What's New, Pussycat?"
Movie Star	Katharine Hepburn, the Pink Panther
Editor	Maxwell Purrkins
Designer	Oscat de la Renta
Poem	"The Three Little Kittens"; "Three Blind Mice"
Charity	the ASPCA
Sculpture	The Sphinx
Book	*First Feline* (what else?)

Having been raised in a political family, I'm probably more goal-directed than other pussy cats. In fact, some consider me more of a *pushy* cat.

But the idea of helping lead the country caused a transformation in my basic behavior philosophy—from a traditional cat-like, ego-centered consciousness to a group consciousness.

I enjoy television. But I'm very particular. I like to wait until Ted Koppel comes on at 11:30. By then, the set is all warmed up and cozy-snuggly.

My favorite hobby is blowing sax—with The Main Man, of course. I love all that cool jazz from the Forties. Guess that makes me a real hep cat.

And sometimes, when he plays, I'll indulge myself with a little s-cat singing.

Like The Main Man, I'm a lefty, and this is probably what surprises tourists most when I give them my autograph.

Basically, I'm like any other cat. I eat. I sleep. I use a litter box and I like it lined with trash paper—speeches by Pat Buchanan, Pat Robertson and *The New York Post.*

The transition from one administration to another is generally slow and deliberate. Only the Washington cat-trepreneurs aren't wasting any time.

The White House chef is working with the transition team on my menu. Other felines are happy with Friskies or canned tuna. I prefer traditional Arkansas catfish. Without any bones.

Transition also involves editing the library. Hey, she may have made a million bucks on it, but what kind of phony publishes a book in her own name that somebody else wrote?

As a cat, I'm more independent. A true freelancer. If there's going to be any book about me, I'll do it myself (except for this one, since I can't draw). Matter of fact, I've already put a few things down on paper.

When they move into new places, cats like to stake out their own territory. Each cat does it differently. I, too, have my own special way.

The housekeepers worry about me shedding hair all over the place. They shouldn't. So maybe it'll be called the Not-Quite-White House. As long as they don't call it anything worse.

And it looks like there'll be a fundamental change in my social life that'll take some getting used to. Before, when I went out catting at night, I did it *alone.* This may make me cat-atonic.

White House security is very tough. When we first arrived I had to get paw printed, ear-marked and photographed for my pussport. And every time I go in or out I have to have a CAT Scan.

In *this* White House, *everybody* is sharp.

GEE, HOW DID THEY KNOW I WAS GOING TO BE AWAY THIS WEEKEND ?
CAMP DUVID

Naturally, I've always liked to climb trees, but it's much more enjoyable around the White House. *Love* that presidential timber!

Hey, look at this: if the former president really thought the economy was not all that bad, why was he growing his own carrots, radishes, tomatoes and corn in the Rose Garden?

I was excited about moving to Washington — and my first glimpse told me that I would really enjoy it.

One night after
we arrived I went
out sight-seeing
and found a
comfortable lap
to snuggle in.
What a great
feeling. Like I
was in the cat-
bird seat.

Washington seems to be a purrfect place for a politicat like me. From what I've seen, it's standard behavior to do a lot of back-scratching, tail-licking and pussy-footing.

Washington is populated mostly by fat cats, who like to throw their weight around . . .

and by bureau-cats . . .

many of whom, as they stay around and develop a taste for power, become auto-cats.

Others dream of reaching a higher level of Washington society, living in Georgetown and becoming aristo-cats.

The whole town is brimming with unbelievable cat-acters. I even met one who claimed he'd spent a lot of time around the former vice-president.

And there's so much going on in Washington. Every day there's a parade—in and out of the Capitol—of lobbyists, PACs, influence peddlers, all prowling on one trail or another.

I'm probably the only one around who's not sniffing for a job. If I was asked to, though, I'd agree to head up the Department of Snoozing/Eating/Playing-With-String/Stretching/Lying-In-The-Sun / And Rubbing Against Legs.

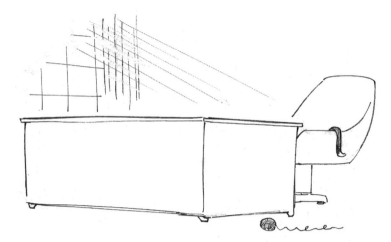

I think one assignment I'll have will be to sit on the window sill in the Oval Office and stare blankly back at The Main Man when he questions the priorities on his cat-alog of national problems. That way I'll be his cat-alyst.

(Living with The Main Man has taught me many things, not the least of which is never to be daunted. No matter how tough the job looks, we believe we *can* do it.)

I'd be interested in chairing special arms reduction talks. Our fundamental question will be: To declaw or not to declaw.

I probably will have a general summit cat-ference to which many special interest groups will be invited.

And while it won't be an official Cabinet position, I might help out by extending greetings to those who come to call.

For the most part, I expect my presence will go unnoticed, except by certain visitors.

I'm constantly learning political concepts. The other day, a container of milk spilled and I soon understood that trickle down theories really *don't* work very well.

Another thing I've learned about politics is that it's advantageous to know how to speak the language of your adversaries.

I'm already on record as being in favor of capital punishment. But I also support prison reform. I say, open the cages, let 'em out, and I'll bite their heads off.

Despite evidence to the contrary, some reports scoff that a cat does not help create a strong presidential image. Republicans, including the former President himself, think dogs are better in the White House. Oh, yeah? Read my clips.

Some Republicats still don't get it.

I'm often asked how I *really* feel about politics.
"No comment."

When Christmas arrived, the family realized that we'd already received what we wanted; Santa Claws came early this year.

Finally, there was the In-augural Ball and it was great. The cat's meow. Friends came to help me celebrate.

And in a gesture of re-cat-ciliation and togeth-erness, we even set a table for some classic old adversaries.

Anyway, that's it for now. Gotta scat. We're looking forward to having a cat-aclysmic, felin-icitous time. God Bless Americat!

Mort Gerberg is a cartoonist and writer widely known for his magazine cartoons, which appear regularly in *Publishers Weekly, The New Yorker* and in *Playboy.* He has drawn several nationally-syndicated comic strips and has written and/or illustrated over 30 books of humor for adults and children. His *Cartooning: The Art and the Business,* published by William Morrow, is the leading instructional-reference work in the field. His most recent book is *Joy in Mudville: The Big Book of Baseball Humor,* with Dick Schaap.

Mr. Gerberg has also written, drawn and performed on television and, with Shari Lewis, on home video. He teaches cartooning at New York City's Parsons School of Design and lectures nationally. Mr. Gerberg lives in New York City with his wife, Judith, their daughter, Lilia and their cat, Pixie.